Children's
PICTURE ATLAS

illustrated by Becky Radtke

ABOUT THIS BOOK

This book is an Atlas or a book of maps.

But what is a map?

A map is a drawing that shows the earth's surface. It helps people understand the different regions of the world and where things are. There are many types of maps that give people different kinds of information about the world. Some maps show how the world is divided up into continents and countries. These maps also may show where large cities, lakes, rivers, oceans and seas are located. Other maps include symbols or pictures that tell about the type of land or climate in each region. Some maps even show animals, products, customs and famous landmarks that can be found in particular areas.

This Atlas contains maps that show the major regions of the world. Each map includes divisions that show countries. Oceans, seas, major rivers and lakes can also be seen on each map.

The regions of the world are covered by many types of land like mountains, valleys, tropical rain forests, deserts, and even tundra (frozen land). You can use the legend, or key, on the next page to see what each symbol means.

The maps in this Atlas even show animals, products, and famous landmarks that can be found in particular areas. You can also use the legend to see what each of these symbols mean.

Throughout this book, you will find "Fun Facts" about each region, and there are also "Atlas Adventures" for you to try.

LEGEND OF SYMBOLS

Topographical

mountains   desert   tundra   rain forest   volcanoes

Animals

snake   grizzly bear   alligator   seal   polar bear   jaguar

giraffe   hippo   lion   gazelle   elephant   zebra

camel   rhino   fox   bull   whale   shark

koala bear   platypus   sheep   penguin   kangaroo

Famous Landmarks

GoldenGate Bridge   Mount Rushmore   Sears Tower   Niagra Falls   Mayan Ruins

Pyramids   Taj Mahal   Big Ben   Eiffel Tower   Motherland Monument

Products

timber   potatoes   wheat   oil

corn   dairy   cotton   citrus

seafood   gold   coffee   cattle

sugar   copper   wine   dates

diamonds   coal   rice   tea

electronics   automobiles   chalk   steel

textiles   butane

World Map

Look at the globe on this page. It shows how the world spins on its axis. It turns around and makes a full circle once every twenty-four hours. The line around the center of the globe is called the equator. It is an imaginary line that divides the earth in half. The top half is called the northern hemisphere; the bottom half is called the southern hemisphere.

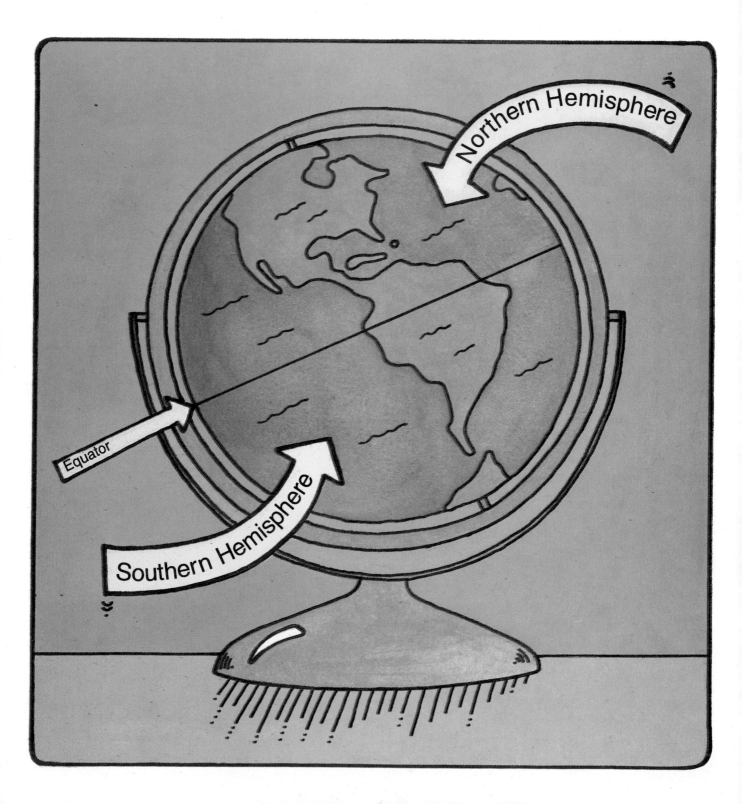

Although the world is round, this map shows what the world would look like if it were flattened out. The regions of the world are shown in different colors and the bodies of water are shown in blue. There is also a compass on this page. It shows the different directions and helps us to locate a particular area. The compass shows north (N), south (S), east (E), and west (W). Use the compass on each page to help find specific places.

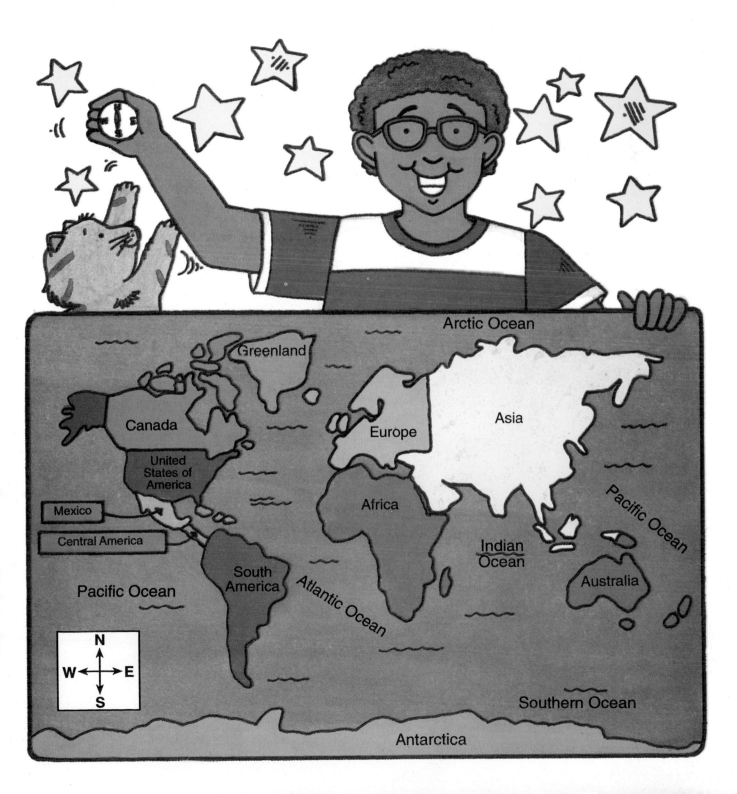

The United States of America

The United States of America, the fourth largest country in the world, was first inhabited by Native American tribes. Over the past several centuries, people from all over the world have come to live in the United States. There are fifty states in the U.S.A.; however, two of these – Alaska and Hawaii – are not connected to the rest of the country by land.

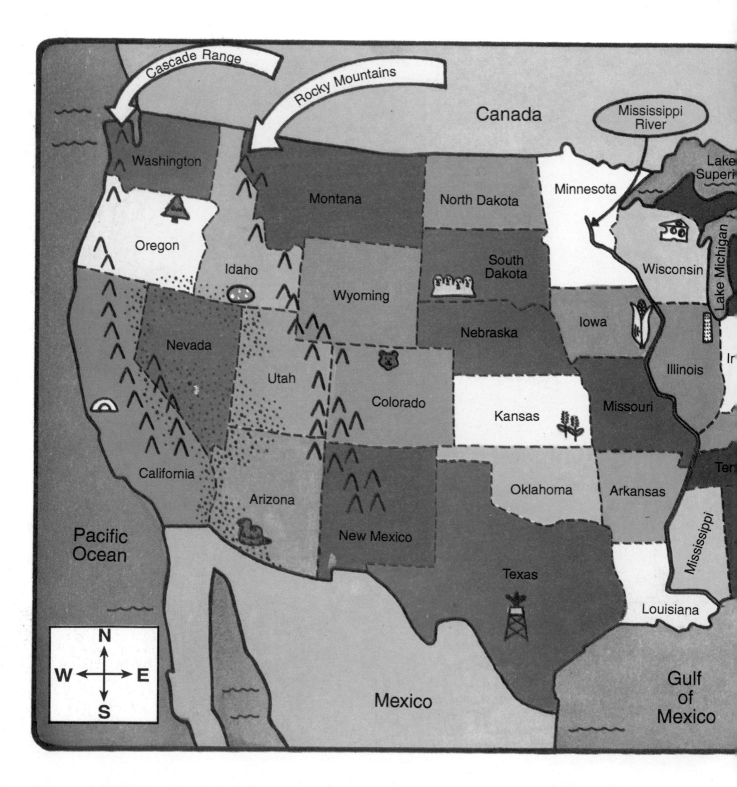

Fun Facts

★ Alaska is the largest state in the U.S.A. but has the smallest population.
★ The longest river is the Mississippi River (about 3,700 miles).
★ The tallest mountain is Mount McKinley in Alaska (20,320 feet).
★ The five Great Lakes are Superior, Michigan, Huron, Erie and Ontario. The largest lake is Michigan (about 22,400 square miles).
★ The tallest mountain is Mount McKinley in Alaska (20,320 feet).
★ The biggest city is New York City which has about 7 million people living in it.

Map

Appalachian Mountains

Lake Ontario

Huron

Lake Erie

Vermont

Maine

New Hampshire

Massachusetts

Rhode Island

Connecticut

New York

Pennsylvania

New Jersey

Ohio

Delaware

West Virginia

Maryland

Virginia

Atlantic Ocean

North Carolina

South Carolina

Hawaii

Georgia

Florida

Mt. McKinley

Alaska

ATLAS ADVENTURES

• How many states border the five Great Lakes?
• How many states does the Mississippi River run through?
• What states are along the Pacific Coast?
• What part of the country has large mountain ranges?
• Can you name three products that come from the United States?
• Are there more mountains in the eastern states or in the western states?

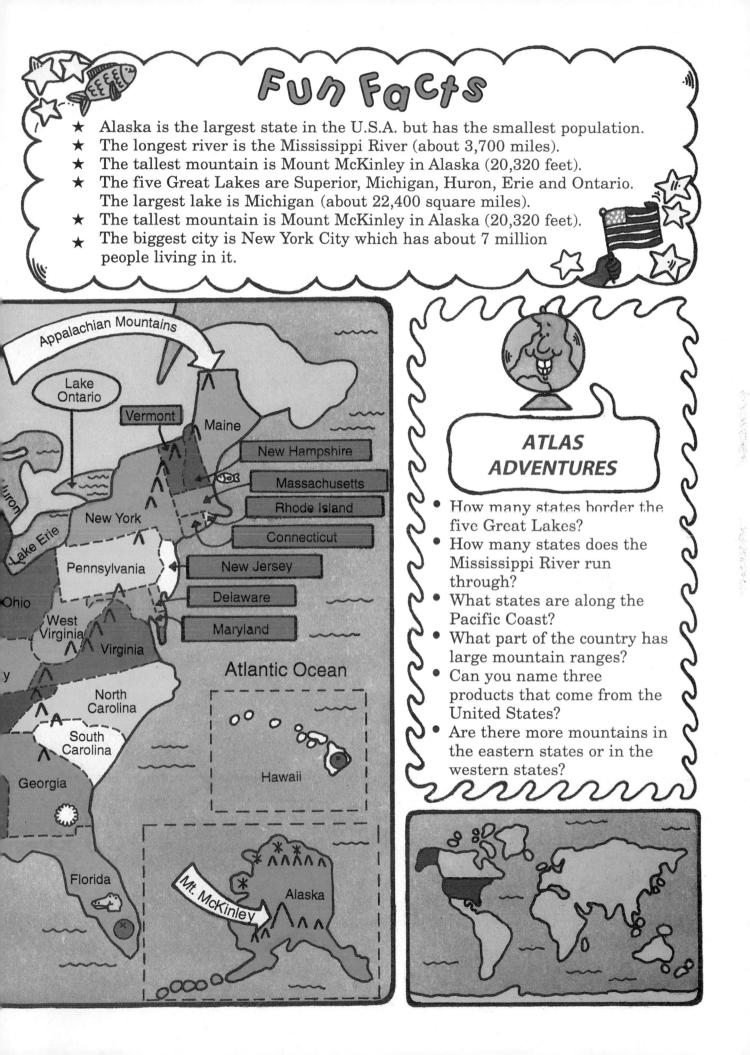

Canada

Part of the North American continent, Canada borders most of the United States. It lies between the Pacific Ocean, the Arctic Ocean and the Atlantic Ocean. Although Canada is the second largest country in the world, most people live near the major cities and many mountainous areas are sparsely populated. Canada is part of the British Commonwealth of Nations, but it is independent and has its own Prime Minister and Parliament. French and English are the two official languages of Canada; most French-speaking Canadians live in Quebec.

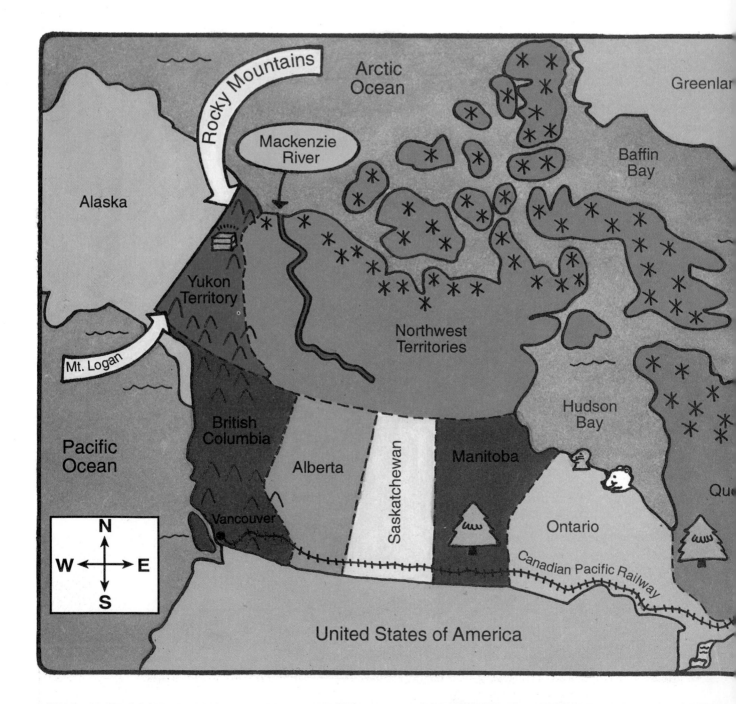

Fun Facts

★ Completed in 1885, the Canadian Pacific Railway runs from eastern to western Canada. It helped to unify the regions into one country. The trip from Montreal to Vancouver is about 2,860 miles.

★ Niagara Falls, the largest waterfall in the world, lies on the border of the United States and Canada. The water power is used to create electricity.

★ Winter sports such as ice hockey are a popular Canadian pastime.

★ The tallest mountain in Canada is Mount Logan in the Yukon Territory (19,500 feet).

★ Some of the natural resources in Canada include silver, gold, oil and lumber. Since Canada is surrounded by so much water, the fishing industry is also quite prosperous.

Atlantic Ocean

Newfoundland

Prince Edward Island

Nova Scotia

New Brunswick

ATLAS ADVENTURES

• Which provinces do you pass through if you travel from Montreal to Vancouver on the Canadian Pacific Railway?

• What provinces border the Hudson Bay?

• The Mackenzie River is the longest river in Canada. Can you find where it begins and ends on the map?

• What ocean is near the coldest climate?

• What provinces border the United States? Look carefully, this is tricky.

Mexico, Central America and South America

Underneath the United States lies the country of Mexico. People usually think of Mexico as being part of North America. South of Mexico lie the countries that make up Central America. These also include the countries of the Caribbean Sea. South America, the fourth largest continent, stretches from above the equator almost to Antarctica. Because of their location near the equator, the countries near the Amazon River are warm and rainy. Chile and areas closer to Antarctica are cold and sometimes stormy.

Areas in Mexico, Central America and the pacific coast of South America are rather mountainous. The Valley along the Amazon River contains the world's largest rain forest. South America also has large grassland areas and even some desert regions.

Fun Facts

★ Completed in 1914, the Panama Canal is a 51 mile canal that connects the Caribbean Sea with the Pacific Ocean. Prior to the building of this canal, ships had to travel all around South America to reach the Pacific Ocean.

★ Brazil is the largest country in South America and the fifth largest country in the world. Brasilia is the capital city of Brazil.

★ Many countries in Central and South America speak Spanish or Portuguese.

ATLAS ADVENTURES

- Find the Panama Canal on the map. Trace your finger around South America to see how a ship had to travel before the Panama Canal was built.
- What countries border Brazil?
- What country is Buenos Aires in?
- What bodies of water surround Mexico and Central America?
- What South American countries do not border the ocean or the sea?
- Through which countries does the equator run?

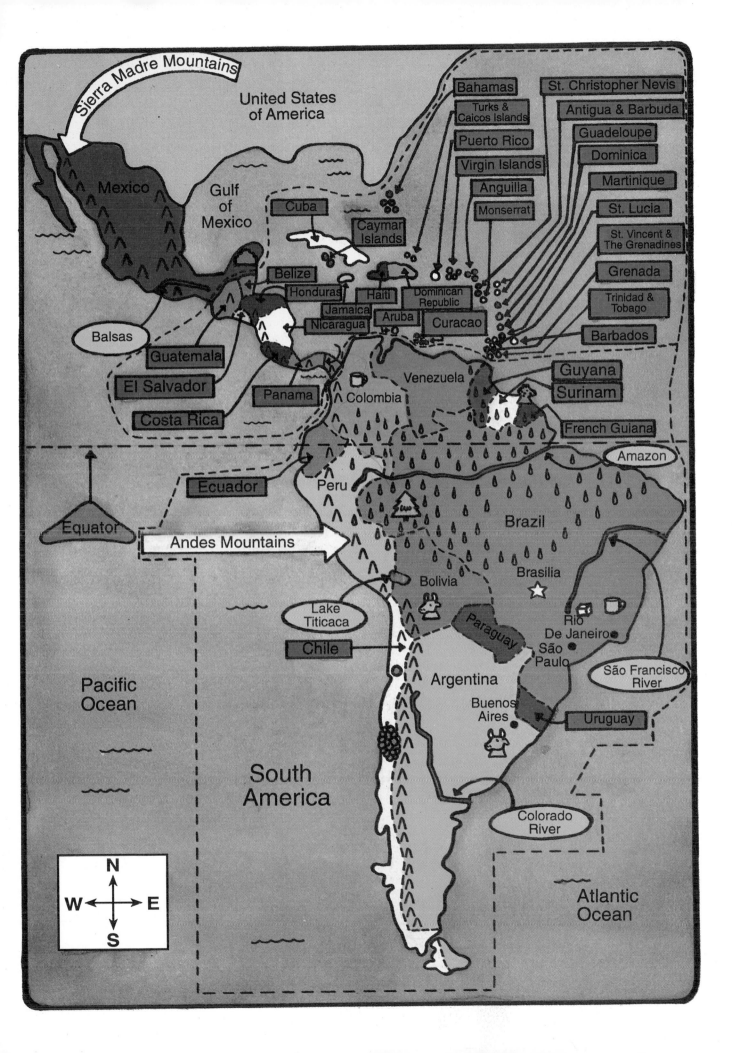

Africa

Africa, the second largest continent in the world, is surrounded by four bodies of water — the Mediterranean Sea, the Red Sea, the Atlantic Ocean and the Indian Ocean. Of the over 50 countries in Africa, many countries are covered by grasslands and rain forests. There are also two deserts in Africa. The Sahara Desert is in the north and the Namib Desert is in the south.

Although many ancient cultures originated in Africa, much of the continent was later colonized by European nations. In recent years the native people in the various countries have achieved independence and created their own new nations.

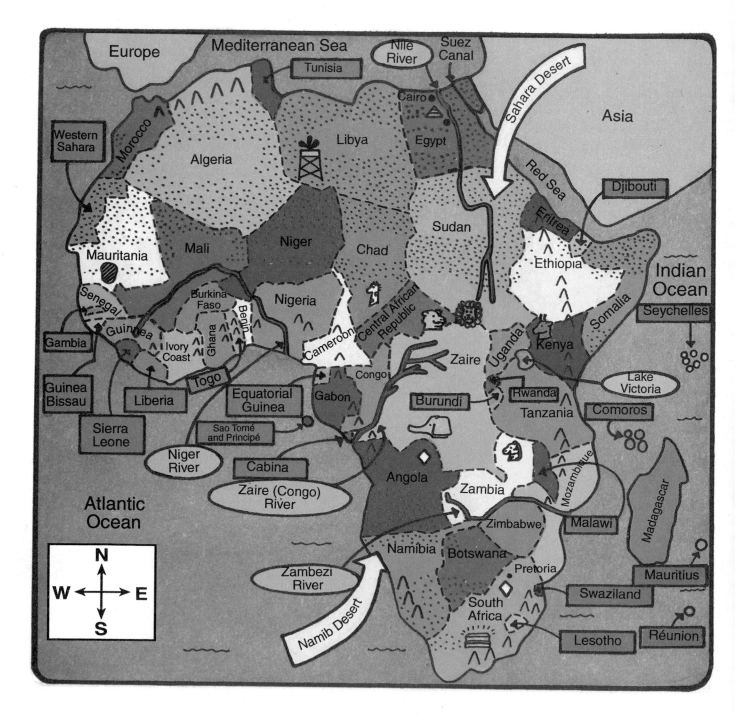

Fun Facts

★ One of the Seven Wonders of the World, the Pyramids and the Sphinx are found in Egypt. The pyramids, built about 4,500 years ago, are tombs built out of heavy stone blocks.

★ Although the world's oldest diamond mines are in Swaziland, the largest diamond, the Cullinan diamond was found in Pretoria, South Africa in 1905. Gold, however, is South Africa's main export.

★ The savannahs of East Africa are the home of many exotic animals such as elephants, giraffes, zebras and lions. These animals were hunted in the past but are now protected in large game reserves.

★ The largest country in Africa is Sudan. The smallest country on the mainland is Gambia but the islands of Seychelles in the Indian Ocean are much smaller.

★ The Suez Canal connects the Mediterranean Sea with the Red Sea. First opened in 1869, this shortened the sea route from Europe to India and the Far East. Prior to the Suez Canal the route went all the way around Africa.

ATLAS ADVENTURES

- Find these four important rivers on the map: Nile, Niger, Zambezi and Zaire.
- What country is the furthest south?
- Lake Victoria is the largest lake in Africa. Find it on the map and name the countries that it is in.
- What countries might you travel through to get from Morocco to Egypt?
- What ocean borders the Namib Desert? Hint: the Namib Desert is in Namibia.
- In what countries are gold and diamonds mined?

Asia

Asia, the largest continent in the world, spans from the cold Arctic Ocean in the north to the warm tropical waters of the Indian Ocean. To the east is the Pacific Ocean and to the west is the Mediterranean and the Red Sea. Although over half of the world's population lives in Asia, they tend to live in crowded more concentrated areas. Much of Asia is mountainous, cold or desert, so there are vast areas that are sparsely inhabited. There are many cultures in Asia even though two countries - China and Russia - cover over half of the land. Although smaller in size, there are many other important countries in Asia.

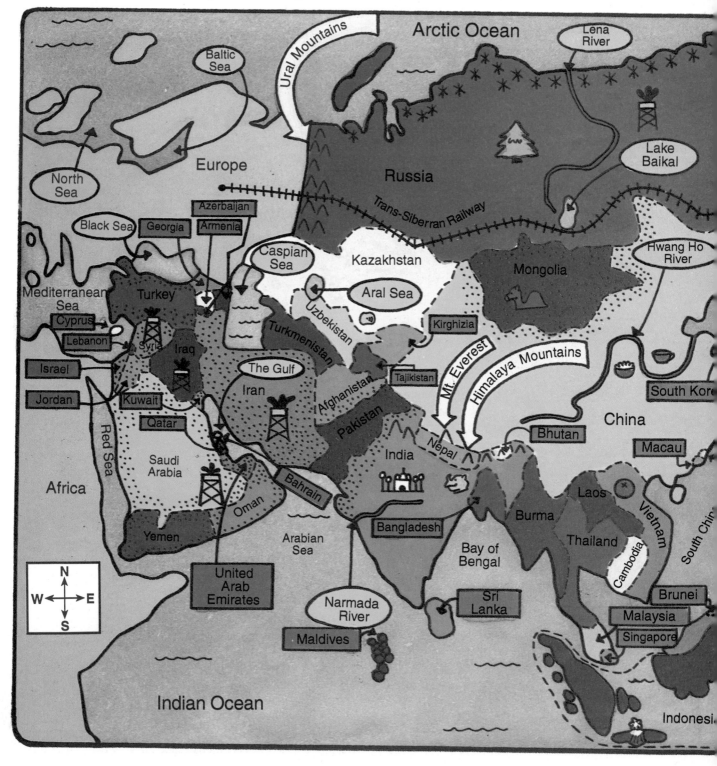

Fun Facts

★ The world's ten highest mountains are in the Himalayan Mountain range. Mount Everest, the highest mountain in Asia (29,028 feet), is on the border between Nepal and Tibet.

★ Russia is so wide, it takes eight days to cross the country by train. Passengers on the world's longest railroad, the Trans-Siberian Railway, change their watches seven times as they cross into new time zones.

ATLAS ADVENTURES

- Russia is the largest country in Asia followed by China. Which country do you think is third?
- Mount Everest is the largest mountain in Nepal and in the world. Find it on the map.
- What country do you cross to get from Korea to Mongolia?
- What country is the furthest north?
- Name two countries that produce oil. Hint: Look in the Middle East.
- What countries associated with Asia are islands?
- What two large countries border Mongolia?
- What countries border Yemen?
- What mainland country is closest to Sri Lanka?

Sea of Okhotsk

Sea of Japan

th Korea

Japan

East China Sea

Taiwan

Hong Kong

Philippines

Pacific Ocean

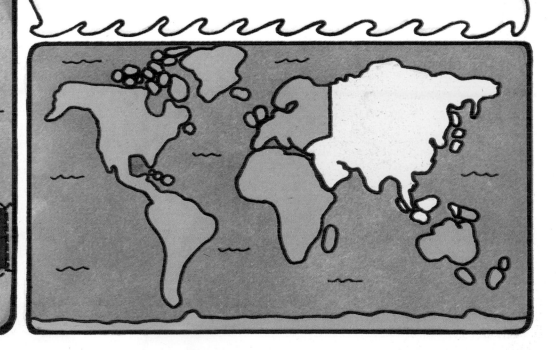

Europe

Although Europe is part of the same land as Asia, it is considered a continent. It is smaller in land area than North America but has a much larger population. The richest farmland, and most densely populated cities are on Europe's central plain, which stretches from Northern France to Russia. Rivers and ports along the coastlines have helped the European nations develop and expand international trade. In 1993 the European community created a single market permitting free trade and allowing the free movement of people and goods.

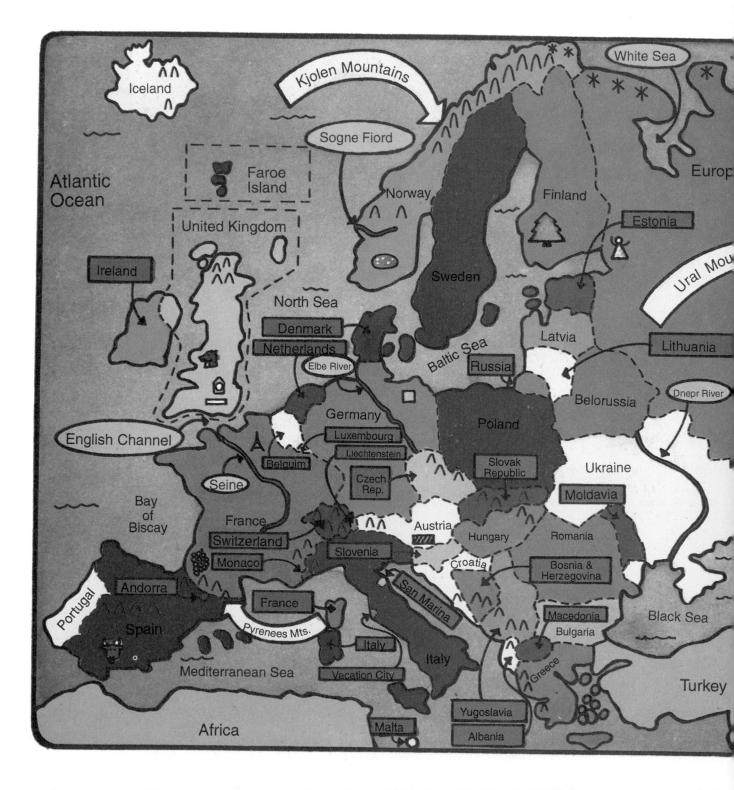

Fun Facts

★ Close to the Arctic Circle, Iceland is the most northern country in Europe.

★ Belgium, the Netherlands and Luxembourg are often referred to Benelux. This name comes from the first two letters of each country's name. These countries are also called "The Low Countries" because much of the land is low lying.

★ France is the largest country in Western Europe. Mont Blanc, in the French Alps is the tallest mountain in Western Europe (over 15,000 feet).

ATLAS ADVENTURES

- What country do you cross to go from France to Portugal?
- What countries border Switzerland?
- What country is the furthest north?
- What country is Big Ben located in?
- Name at least two countries that are on the Mediterranean Sea.
- What country is shaped like a boot?
- How many different Seas can you find on the map?
- What country is the Seine River in?
- What is the longest mountain range?
- What country is the Eiffel Tower located in?
- What country has a large timber resource?

Caspian Sea

N
W — E
S

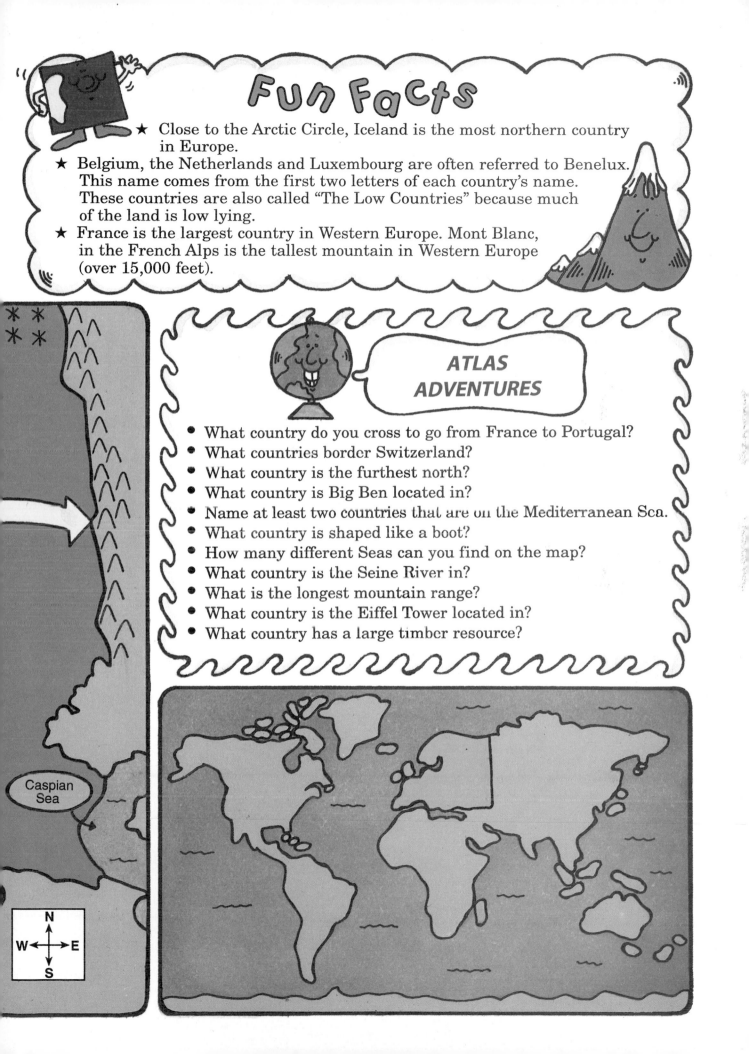

Oceania

Australia, New Zealand and the thousands of islands south and east of Asia form a region called Oceania or Australasia. Australia is the smallest continent in the world but it is also the largest island in the world. It lies south of the equator and sometimes is referred to as the area "down under". Most of the people live in cities along the coast of Australia. New Zealand and the Pacific Islands are divided into three groups based on the origins of its earliest inhabitants. New Zealand is considered to be part of Polynesia; the Caroline Islands and Kirbati are part of Micronesia; Fiji and Papua New Guinea are part of Melanesia. The distances between countries in Oceania are very large.

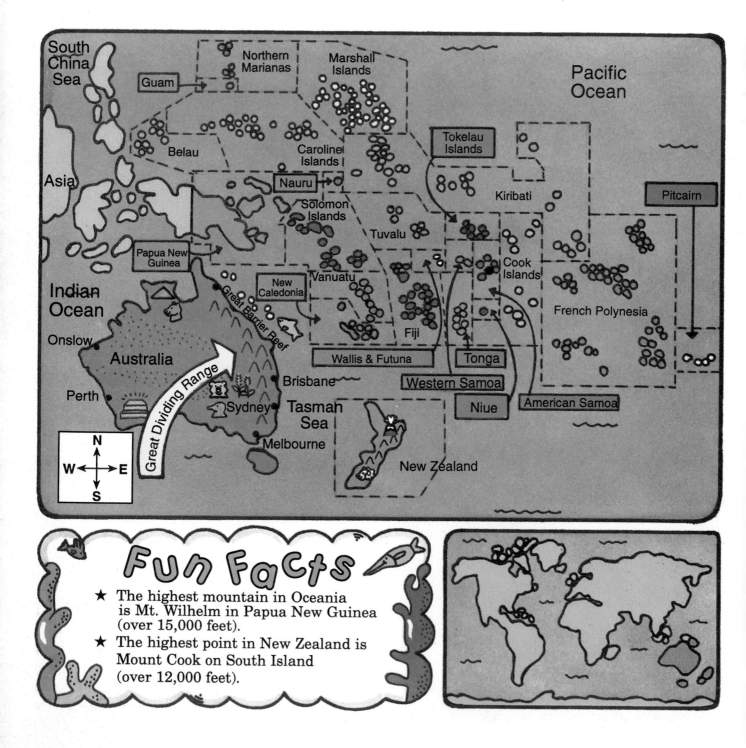

Fun Facts

★ The highest mountain in Oceania is Mt. Wilhelm in Papua New Guinea (over 15,000 feet).

★ The highest point in New Zealand is Mount Cook on South Island (over 12,000 feet).

Antarctica

Antarctica, the icy region surrounding the South Pole, is the sixth largest continent in the world. Since it is extremely cold and most of the world's ice and snow is in Antarctica, no population has ever lived there permanently. Scientists often travel to the Antarctic to study weather, animal life and other things in the environment.

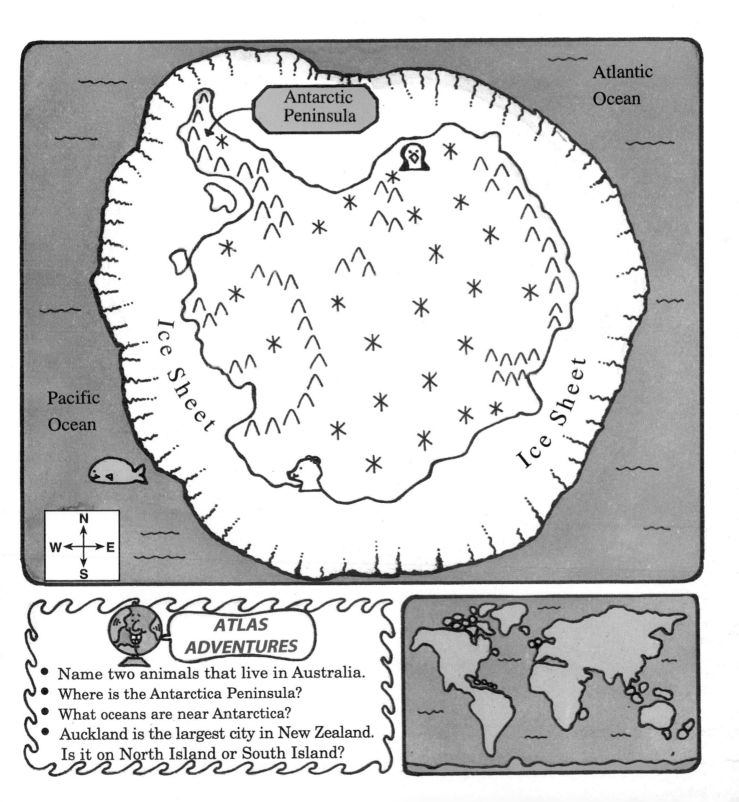

Atlantic Ocean

Antarctic Peninsula

Pacific Ocean

Ice Sheet

Ice Sheet

N
W · E
S

ATLAS ADVENTURES

- Name two animals that live in Australia.
- Where is the Antarctica Peninsula?
- What oceans are near Antarctica?
- Auckland is the largest city in New Zealand. Is it on North Island or South Island?

You have just read about many places in the world. There are many ways that you can find out more about the world. Here are some ideas.

Make a Family Tree

Find out where your family comes from. Start by writing down your name and where you were born. Then find out where your parents came from and write that down. Keep asking questions and record the answers. Find out where your parent's parents came from and go back as many generations as you can. Find each person's place of birth on the maps in this book.

Collect Stamps from Around the World

Start a stamp collection. You can learn about a country from it's stamps. There might be a flag from a particular nation or something relating to the history of a country. Some stamps show political figures or famous individuals. You might also choose to collect stamps that have a special topic. Create a collection of stamps that show something about sports or nature. After you have collected several stamps, find the country that each stamp is from in this book.

What We Own

There are many products that are made in one country and then used in a different country. This atlas shows where some products come from. Look through this book to get some ideas. Then walk around your house and find items that are made in different countries. Remember that some products come from more than one place in the world. Make a list of all the items you find and the country each one comes from. Here's a hint – look in the kitchen!

Francs, Dollars and Yen

Starting a coin collection is a terrific way to find out about different coutries. Each country has its own monetary system to learn about. You can discover which countries use francs, dollars, yen, pesos, lira, pounds and marks. As you look at each type of money, you may learn about famous people and places in each country. Different languages and historical events may also be depicted on different currencies.

Write The United Nations

The United Nations was created as an institution that would represent the many countries of the world and help create world peace. You can write to the United Nations for more information about the world or about a particular country. You can also write to a specific consulate or tourist information bureau to receive additional information about a particular country.

UNITED NATIONS
RE: CHILDREN
NEW YORK , NY 10017
USA